PIANO SOLO

PRINCE OF PERSIA
THE SANDS OF TIME

S0-BNJ-176

MUSIC COMPOSED BY
HARRY GREGSON-WILLIAMS

ISBN 978-1-4234-9662-5

WONDERLAND MUSIC COMPANY

DISTRIBUTED BY

HAL•LEONARD®
CORPORATION

7777 W. BLUEMOUND RD. P.O. BOX 13819 MILWAUKEE, WI 53213

In Australia Contact:
Hal Leonard Australia Pty. Ltd.
4 Lentara Court
Cheltenham, Victoria, 3192 Australia
Email: ausadmin@halleonard.com.au

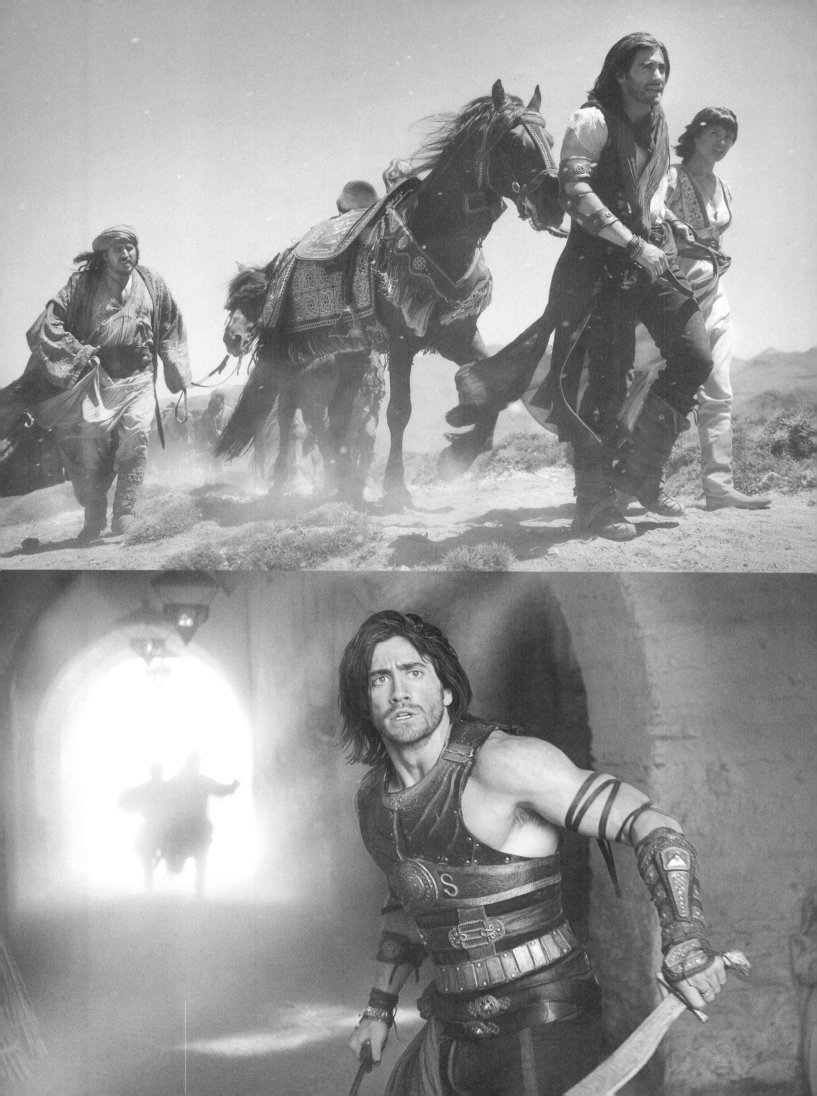

THE PRINCE OF PERSIA

Music by
HARRY GREGSON-WILLIAMS

cresc. poco a poco

mf

f

8va - - - - - - - - - - - - - - - - - - -

THE KING AND HIS SONS

Music by
HARRY GREGSON-WILLIAMS

DASTAN AND TAMINA ESCAPE

Music by
HARRY GREGSON-WILLIAMS

Moderately fast

OSTRICH RACE

Music by
HARRY GREGSON-WILLIAMS

Quickly, in 1

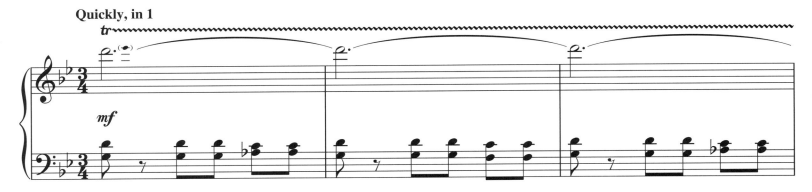

21

TRUSTING NIZAM

Music by
HARRY GREGSON-WILLIAMS

THE PASSAGES

Music by
HARRY GREGSON-WILLIAMS

Moderately slow

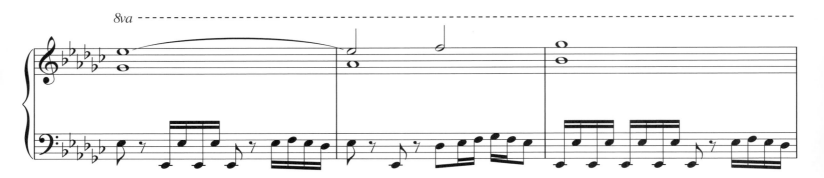

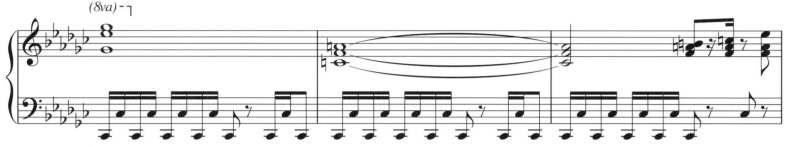

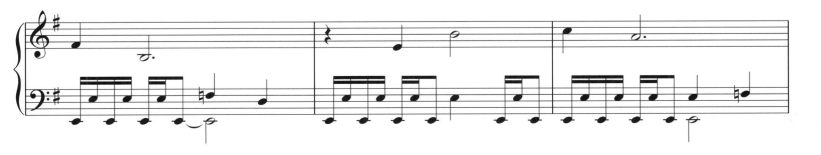

Moderately slow

Slightly faster

mp

cresc. e accel.

8vb

THE SANDS OF TIME

Music by
HARRY GREGSON-WILLIAMS

Moderately, in 2

DESTINY

Music by
HARRY GREGSON-WILLIAMS

Slowly, expressively

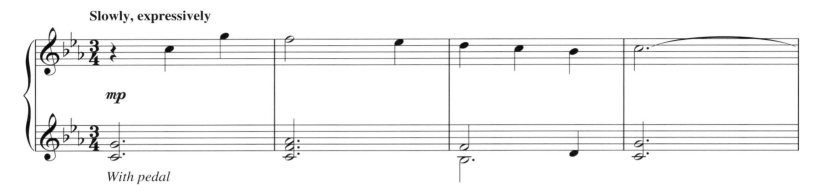

mp

With pedal

Moderately slow

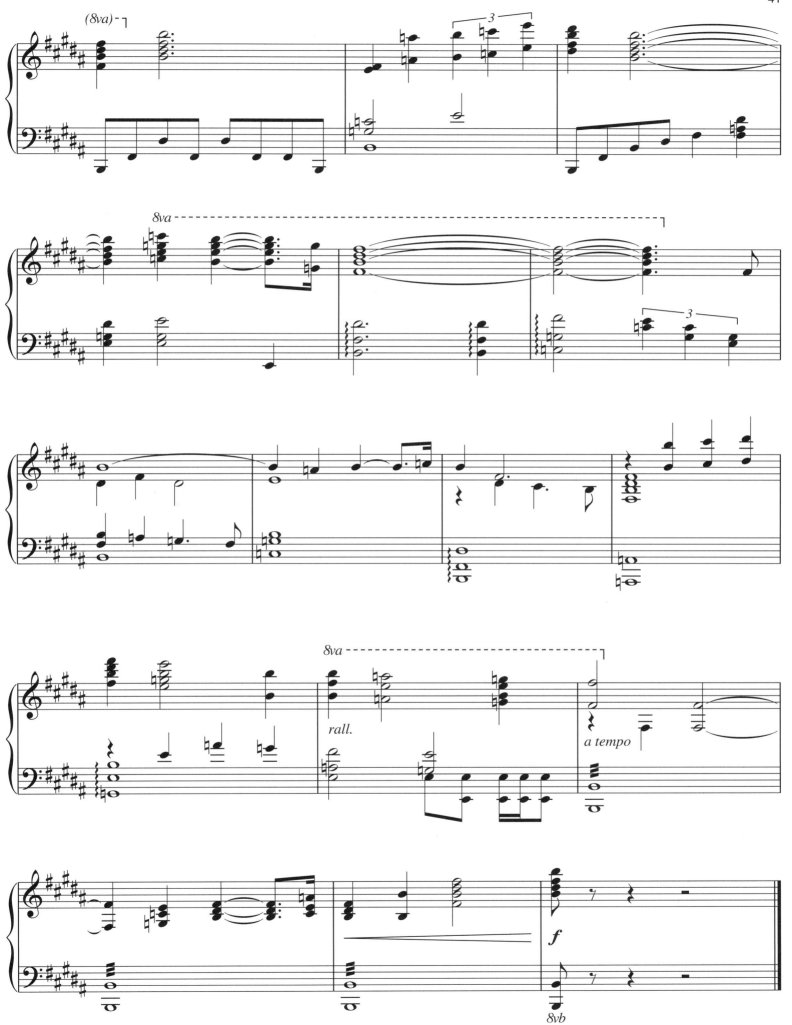

I REMAIN

Words and Music by ALANIS MORISSETTE
and MIKE ELIZONDO

Oh.

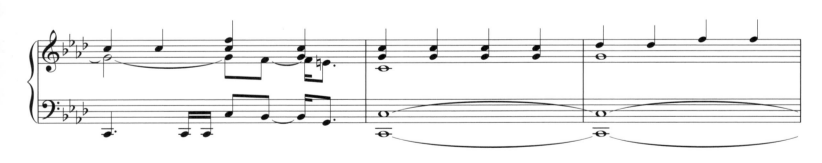

Repeat and Fade

Optional Ending

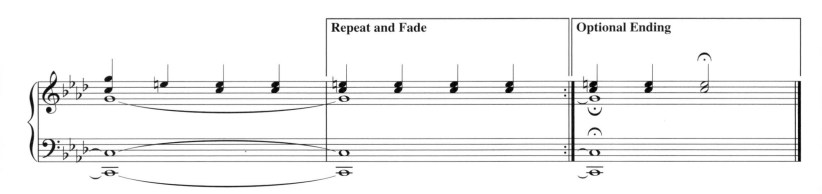